Why Do We Need Soil?

Kelley MacAulay

Crabtree Publishing Company
www.crabtreebooks.com

Author
Kelley MacAulay

Publishing plan research and development
Reagan Miller

Notes to adults
Reagan Miller

Editor
Crystal Sikkens

Proofreader
Wendy Scavuzzo

Design
Tammy McGarr

Photo research
Tammy McGarr, Crystal Sikkens

**Production coordinator
and prepress technician**
Tammy McGarr

Print coordinator
Margaret Amy Salter

Photographs
iStockphoto: redmal: pages 16, 24
Thinkstock: pages 22, 24
All other images by Shutterstock

Library and Archives Canada Cataloguing in Publication

MacAulay, Kelley, author
    Why do we need soil / Kelley MacAulay.

(Natural resources close-up)
Includes index.
Issued in print and electronic formats.
ISBN 978-0-7787-0493-5 (bound).--ISBN 978-0-7787-0497-3 (pbk.).--
ISBN 978-1-4271-8218-0 (html).--ISBN 978-1-4271-8222-7 (pdf)

    1. Soils--Juvenile literature. I. Title.

S591.3.M23 2014   j631.4   C2014-900382-X
                                C2014-900383-8

Library of Congress Cataloging-in-Publication Data

MacAulay, Kelley, author.
    Why do we need soil? / Kelley MacAulay.
      pages cm. -- (Natural resources close-up)
    Includes index.
    ISBN 978-0-7787-0493-5 (reinforced library binding : alk. paper) -- ISBN 978-
0-7787-0497-3 (pbk. : alk. paper) -- ISBN 978-1-4271-8218-0 (electronic html)
-- ISBN 978-1-4271-8222-7 (electronic pdf)
    1. Soils--Juvenile literature. 2. Natural resources--Juvenile literature. I. Title.

S591.3.M33 2014
631.4--dc23
                    2014002280

Crabtree Publishing Company

www.crabtreebooks.com   1-800-387-7650

Printed in the USA/052014/SN20140313

**Published in Canada
Crabtree Publishing**
616 Welland Ave.
St. Catharines, Ontario
L2M 5V6

**Published in the United States
Crabtree Publishing**
PMB 59051
350 Fifth Avenue, 59th Floor
New York, New York 10118

**Published in the United Kingdom
Crabtree Publishing**
Maritime House
Basin Road North, Hove
BN41 1WR

**Published in Australia
Crabtree Publishing**
3 Charles Street
Coburg North
VIC 3058

Contents

Resources from nature

People are living things. Some of the things we need to stay alive can be found in nature. Natural resources are the things found in nature that people use.

What do you think?

Plants, sunlight, air, and water are some of Earth's important natural resources. How do we use these natural resources?

What is soil?

Have you ever searched for buried treasure in your backyard? If you have, you were digging in soil! Soil is another important natural resource that all living things need.

soil

Soil is a layer of loose material. It covers most of the land on Earth. It is found in forests, deserts, and fields. It is even found on the bottoms of oceans, rivers, and lakes.

Living and non-living

There are living and non-living things in soil. Soil is made up of bits of rock mixed with water and air. In soil there is also material from dead plants and animals.

dead plants

Billions of tiny living things called organisms live in soil! Organisms break down dead animals and plants. The dead plants and animals then become part of the soil.

Give and take

Dead animals and plants add nutrients to soil. Nutrients keep living things healthy. Nutrients in soil are used by living plants and animals. Plants take in nutrients from the soil through their **roots**.

roots

Animals get nutrients from the soil by eating plants or eating other animals that eat plants. Animal droppings then add nutrients back to the soil.

Making new soil

Soil forms very slowly. It can take hundreds of years for one inch (2.5 centimeters) of new soil to form! New soil is formed when rocks break down into tiny pieces. This can happen when rocks are hit by wind and rain.

Did you know plants can also break rocks? Small plants grow in rock cracks. The plants break the rocks into pieces as they grow bigger.

Types of Soil

Where and how soil is formed can create different types. **Sandy soil** is a type of soil that holds little water. It is light brown. Few plants grow in sandy soil.

sandy soil

Clay soil holds a lot of water. It is sticky. Strong trees can grow in clay soil.

clay soil

Loam soil is the best type of soil for growing plants. It holds just enough water. It has a lot of nutrients.

loam soil

Living in soil

Plants send their roots deep into the soil. Roots hold the plants in place. Roots take in water and nutrients from the soil. Full-grown plants drop **seeds** in the soil. The seeds grow into new plants.

new plant

seed

roots

Many animals and insects live in soil. If you dig in soil you may find earthworms. Earthworms are important soil animals! They move nutrients through the soil. They also dig holes in the soil which let in air and water.

An important resource

People use different types of soil to make many useful things. Sandy soil can be used to make glass. Clay soil can be mixed with water to form bricks. Bricks are used to build people's homes.

clay bricks

clay soil

corn field

What do you **think?**

People grow many plants for food in soil. Plants grown for food are called **crops**. Corn, wheat, and carrots are crops. Besides soil, what other natural resource do crops need to grow?

Losing soil

Trees depend on soil to grow, but soil depends on trees, too! Trees block the wind from blowing soil away. When trees are cut down, soil is lost. Without soil, plants and many animals would have nowhere to live.

You can protect soil by saving trees! Every piece of paper you use is made from trees. Always recycle paper instead of throwing it out. To recycle is to take something old and make it into something new.

What do you think?

People need soil, too. In what ways do people use soil? How would losing soil change the way people live?

recycle bin

Reducing pollution

All living things need natural resources.
Pollution damages natural resources.
Pollution is garbage and chemicals on
the land and in the air and water.

Garbage and chemicals on the ground can leak into soil and damage it. By picking up garbage and recycling, we are reducing, or cutting down, the amount of pollution on Earth.

What do you think?

Cars and trucks add pollution to the air. How can you and your family reduce air pollution?

Words to know

 **clay soil** 15, 18

 **crops** 19

 loam soil 15

 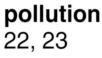 **pollution** 22, 23

 roots 10, 16

 **sandy soil** 14, 18

seeds 16

Activity and notes to adults

This activity encourages children to get their hands dirty —literally!

Materials: Samples of sandy soil, clay soil, and loam; three pieces of white paper; magnifying glass

1. Review the content on pages 14–15.
2. Scoop samples of each soil type onto white pieces of paper. Do not identify the soil samples.
3. Ask readers to use their senses of sight and touch to learn about their soil samples.
4. Children can use a magnifying glass to closely examine each sample. They can touch the soil with their hands.
5. Ask children to name the type of soil in each sample. Encourage children to explain their answers based on what they learned in the book. (Sandy soil is light brown and holds little water. Clay soil is darker than sandy soil. Clay soil holds a lot of water and is sticky. Loam is dark brown and holds more water than sandy soil but less water than clay soil.)

Ask:
• Which soil sample would you use to plant a vegetable garden? Why?
• Which soil sample would you use to make building materials? Why?

Possible extension:
• Try to identify the soil types by touch only.

Learning More

Books

Dig In!: Learn about Dirt by Pamela Hall. Child's World, 2010.

Soil by Sally M. Walker. Lerner Publications, 2007.

Soil Basics by Mari Schuh. Capstone Publishing Company, 2010.

Websites

This site features games, hands-on activities, and a printable book about conservation.
www.soils4kids.org/k-4

This site shows children different soil levels and the organisms living in each.
http://school.discoveryeducation.com/schooladventures/soil/